ICONS

SELENA GOMEZ

BY BETH GOTTLIEB

Enslow PUBLISHING

Please visit our website, www.enslow.com.
For a free color catalog of all our high-quality books, call toll free 1-800-398-2504 or fax 1-877-980-4454.

Library of Congress Cataloging-in-Publication Data
Names: Gottlieb, Beth, author.
Title: Selena Gomez / Beth Gottlieb.
Description: Buffalo : Enslow Publishing, 2025. | Series: Icons | Includes index.
Identifiers: LCCN 2023050728 | ISBN 9781978540194 (library binding) | ISBN 9781978540187 (paperback) | ISBN 9781978540200 (ebook)
Subjects: LCSH: Gomez, Selena, 1992–Juvenile literature. | Actors–United States–Biography–Juvenile literature. | Singers–United States–Biography–Juvenile literature.
Classification: LCC PN2287.G585 G68 2025 | DDC 791.4302/8092 [B]–dc23/eng/20231101
LC record available at https://lccn.loc.gov/2023050728

Published in 2025 by
Enslow Publishing
2544 Clinton Street
Buffalo, NY 14224

Portions of this work were originally authored by Maria Nelson and published as *Selena Gomez*.
All new material in this edition is authored by Beth Gottlieb.

Designer: Tanya Dellaccio Keeney
Editor: Kristen Rajczak Nelson

Photo credits: Cover, p. 19 Tinseltown/Shutterstock.com; p. 5 DFree/Shutterstock.com; p. 7 The Photo Access/Alamy.com; pp. 8, 9, 13 s_bukley/Shutterstock.com; pp. 11, 15, 21, 29 Kathy Hutchins/Shutterstock.com; p. 17 ZUMA Press, Inc./Alamy.com; p. 23 Frylodi/Shutterstock.com; p. 25 Album/Alamy.com; p. 27 DFree/Shutterstock.com.

Printed in the United States of America

CPSIA compliance information: Batch #CSENS25: For further information contact Enslow Publishing, at 1-800-398-2504.

Contents

Words in the glossary appear in **bold** the first time they are used in the text.

Icon for Good

Selena Gomez is truly an **icon**. From starring in hit shows to selling millions of albums, Selena has accomplished a lot—but her goals go beyond music and acting. Selena wants to help her fans find confidence, mental well-being, and their own **rare** beauty.

ICONIC!

Selena is one of the most-followed people on Instagram. She's the most-followed woman as of early 2024!

Selena's Start

Selena was born in Texas on July 22, 1992. Her parents named her after the famous Mexican American singer Selena Quintanilla-Pérez. Selena's mom and dad didn't stay together. Selena lived with her mom, Mandy Teefey.

ICONIC!

*Selena's dad's family is Mexican American. She spoke Spanish with her grandparents when she was young, but she lost her **fluency** after starting school.*

A Rising Star

Selena started acting at just 7 years old. Her first big acting job was on the show *Barney & Friends*. In 2006, Selena appeared on the Disney Channel for the first time. The next year, she began starring as a young witch named Alex on *Wizards of Waverly Place*.

Wizards of Wavery Place Cast

ICONIC!

Selena also sang the theme song for Wizards of Waverly Place*!*

In 2009, Selena's band, Selena Gomez and the Scene, released their first album, *Kiss & Tell*. They released *A Year Without Rain* the following year! The first items from Selena's clothing line, Dream Out Loud, came out in 2010 too.

ICONIC!

Selena became an ambassador for the United Nations Children's Fund (UNICEF) in 2009. She raises money to help children all over the world.

Selena Gomez and the Scene

While Selena was on the Disney Channel, there was a lot of pressure for her to look and act just right. In 2012, *Wizards of Waverly Place* finished airing. Selena began choosing parts that were different from Alex. She wanted to show her acting talent!

ICONIC!

Selena also worked on voice acting. She started voicing Mavis in the Hotel Transylvania ***movies in 2012.***

Going Solo

The last Selena Gomez and the Scene album came out in 2011. Selena was ready to make music of her own. *Stars Dance,* Selena's first solo album, came out in 2013. During the **tour**, Selena wasn't feeling well. She canceled the end of the tour.

ICONIC!

Selena has an illness called lupus that caused some of her problems on tour. Lupus very often causes kidney problems in women who have it.

Selena worked to get well, and she continued to make music. In 2015, she put out another solo album, *Revival.* Selena felt more in control of her own **image** and her music. She co-wrote many songs on the album, as well as produced it.

ICONIC!

Revival *features "Good for You," a song with A$AP Rocky. Selena has collaborated, or worked, with Coldplay, Marshmello, BLACKPINK, and Rema, among others.*

Tough Times

Still, Selena wasn't healthy. She canceled the end of the Revival Tour too. In 2017, she had to have a kidney **transplant** because of problems that came with having lupus. Then, in 2018, she found out she had **bipolar disorder**.

ICONIC!

Selena talked about her health, including her mental health challenges, in Selena Gomez: My Mind & Me, *which came out in 2022.*

She's No. 1!

Selena's song "Lose You to Love Me" hit No. 1 on the *Billboard* charts in October 2019. It was her first No. 1 song! The song was on her third solo album *Rare*. Many of the songs were about the hard times she had been going through.

ICONIC!

Rare *came out in January 2020. It was No. 1 on the* Billboard *albums chart its first week!*

Selena's beauty company, Rare Beauty, also launched in 2020. Selena wanted Rare Beauty to be more than a makeup brand. Part of the company, the Rare Impact Fund, works to raise money for mental health services and education for young people.

ICONIC!

Rare Beauty is named for Selena's song "Rare." She also has that word tattooed on her neck!

SKINCARE
Rare Beauty
BY SELENA GOMEZ
"This is makeup made to feel good in."
Rare Beauty
Rare Beauty
ONLY AT SEPHORA
Rare Beauty
BY SELENA GOMEZ
ONLY AT SEPHORA
Rare Beauty
BY SELENA GOMEZ
"This is makeup made to feel good in."
Rare Beauty
Rare Beauty
ONLY AT SEPHORA
POWER

Star on Screen

Selena + Chef began airing in late 2020. Selena met famous chefs and learned how to cook! In 2023, Selena began appearing on Food Network too. She spent even more time in the kitchen with well-known chefs on her Food Network shows.

ICONIC!

Selena put out a Spanish album **Revelación** ***in 2021. She worked with a Spanish coach. She said singing in Spanish was easier than speaking it!***

Selena teamed up with comedy icons Martin Short and Steve Martin for *Only Murders in the Building*, which first came out in 2021. Selena plays Mabel. Fans loved the fun and mysteries on the show.

ICONIC!

Selena has said working with Martin Short and Steve Martin helped "sharpen" her comedy skills: "I hope to be as funny as they are one day."

Martin Short

Still Rising

Selena has said that her next album may be her last! She does want to keep acting though. Selena's successes show her fans that challenges can be overcome. What will this icon do next?

ICONIC!

Selena told Vanity Fair *in 2023: "I'd rather be remembered for my heart than anything else."*

Timeline

1992	*Selena is born on July 22.*
2002-2004	*She appears on* Barney and Friends.
2007	Wizards of Waverly Place *starts.*
2009	Kiss & Tell *comes out.*
2010	A Year Without Rain *comes out.*
2012	Wizards of Waverly Place *finishes airing.*
2013	Stars Dance, *Selena's first solo album, comes out.*
2015	Revival *comes out.*
2017	*Selena has a kidney transplant.*
2020	Rare *comes out. Rare Beauty launches.*
2021	*Selena begins starring in* Only Murders in the Building.
2022	Selena Gomez: My Mind & Me *comes out.*

For More Information

BOOKS

Andral, Dolores. *What You Never Knew About Selena Gomez*. Oxford, UK: Raintree, 2024.

Kawa, Katie. *Selena Gomez: Making a Difference as a Singer and Actress*. Buffalo, NY: KidHaven Publishing, 2024.

WEBSITES

Selena Gomez
www.imdb.com/name/nm1411125/
Catch up on Selena's movies and TV shows.

Selena Gomez's Official Website
selenagomez.com
Find out the latest news about Selena.

Publisher's note to educators and parents: Our editors have carefully reviewed these websites to ensure that they are suitable for students. Many websites change frequently, however, and we cannot guarantee that a site's future contents will continue to meet our high standards of quality and educational value. Be advised that students should be closely supervised whenever they access the internet.

Glossary

ambassador: A person who acts for a group.

bipolar disorder: A mental health condition in which a person goes from being really happy to really sad fast.

fluency: The ability to speak with ease.

icon: A person who has a lot of success and is admired by many.

image: The idea people have about someone or something.

rare: Not common. Also, special.

tour: A series of concerts that happen in different places over a period of time.

transplant: A medical operation in which a sick organ is removed from the body of one person and replaced by a healthy organ from the body of another person.

Index